Stonecutter

How to resolve discontentment and reclaim meaning at work and in life!

Dr. Albert Kim
Illust by Yuna Joe

Stonecutter

Introduction

"The perfect straight line forms a circle."

In the story, Stonecutter, Tiberius suffers. He suffers because he could only see the world as the "corporate ladder," where one must grab onto the nearest rung and desperately try to climb up to the top.

The Zero-Sum Game—Rock, Paper, Scissors

The ancient game of Rock-Paper-Scissors was mentioned as early as Ming Dynasty by Xie Zhaozhi in his book *Wuzazu.* In this game, a single-step distinction makes it as if one entity is "obviously" more powerful than the other.

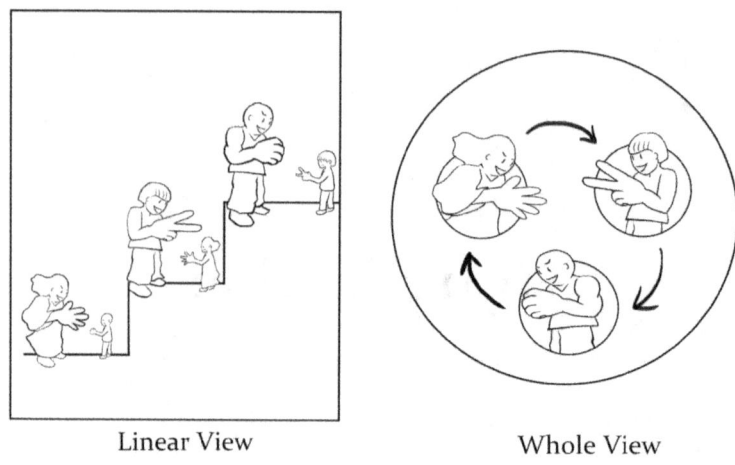

Linear View   Whole View

Figure 2. The zero-sum game of Rock, Paper and Scissors.

In the Linear View (Figure 2), it apears that the Rock sits helplessly at the bottom of the *Power Stairway*.

The Rock is clearly beaten by the more powerful Cloth (Paper) as the Rock (Stone) can be trapped inside a Cloth bag. However, the powerful Cloth (Paper) is easily beaten by the Scissors as they can cut and shape the Cloth any which way.

However, the Scissors — so far the most powerful entity—is easily beaten by the former "bottom-dwelling" Rock as the Rock can break the Scissors. This relationship between the Rock, Paper and Scissors leads to a *conundrum!* The Rock sits at the very bottom *also* sits at the very top!

How can the Rock be the weakest, and at the same time, the strongest? This conundrum naturally resolves when the head (the strongest, which is the Rock) and tail (the weakest, which is also the Rock) are joined. And we can see now, the true relationship between them is not *linear,* but *circular* as shown in the Whole View (Figure 2).

Tiberius Gets "Trapped" in the Linear View

In the beginning, Tiberius sees some individuals as more powerful than he was because of his narrow scope of view. He believes that he would be happier if he were the *other* person, who is believed to have more power. This viewpoint leads him to lose meaning and contentment at work and in life.

Previous to this, he had a chance encounter with a spiritual master who taught him how to manifest what he desires—to become a Master Stonecutter.

Applying that teaching, he accomplishes what would normally be not possible. He climbs up the ladder of hierarchy vigorously! He gets the first-hand experience of the various human and nonhuman positions of power—the Master Stonecutter, the Wealthy Merchant, the

Sun, the Cloud, the Wind, and finally the Giant Rock—only to discover that he comes back full circle to where he had started—the Stonecutter. The rise in the "corporate ladder" only turns out to be a game of *cat chasing its own tail*, ultimately proving itself to be a distraction.

The Solution to Loss of Meaning is the *Acceptance* of the Now

I was hiking near Carson City, Nevada. The rolling hills seen from the highway whispered to me a promised for an easy hike. I pulled the car over, and walked up the hill only to realize how challenging the hike really turned out to be.

The terrain that once appeared smooth from a distance was covered with rough vegetations that constantly caught my feet and tested my balance. I realized that if a mountain lion decided to have me for lunch, it would be difficult to hike away fast enough, let alone running.

Grass *isn't* always greener on the other side of the fence, regardless how much it may appear to be. Grass only *appears* to be greener because it is seen from a distance. Distance tends to smooth out much of the finer details of the trials and... *inspirations* that had taken place.

When awareness is not mature, humans engage in various forms of *resistance*—such as denying the reality of the situation, becoming angry at the world, begging someone to come and alter the reality, or despairing and falling into a depression because they are trapped in an unwanted situation.

Elizabeth Kubler-Ross has stated that acceptance comes *after* depression. And it is acceptance that dissolves ignorance and gives rise to fuller awareness. In fact, the adage, "This too shall pass!" is only true when acceptance falls into its proper place. Without acceptance, the event remains in the darkness of ignorance and therefore, suffering.

The Invisible Cup

The world is forever pouring down raindrops of wealth and poverty; happiness and sadness; grandeur and pettiness; freedom and restraint; health and illness; friendship and enmity; mastery and incompetence; wisdom and foolishness; and winning and losing.

In fact, the universe is *pouring down* all those and more in the Now at this very moment. Yet we are given but a tiny cup that can hold only very little. Some develop a habit of collecting items indiscriminately, simply taking what comes along their way, quickly filling up the precious space in the cup.

Indiscriminate taking isn't the acceptance this story is describing.

Indiscriminate taking is a thoughtless surrendering of one's prerogative—the freedom to make a choice.

Acceptance is the proactive. It is assessing what is available Now, and then carefully choosing.

The Path to Meaning and Contentment

Meaning and Contentment is the *symptom* of one walking the higher path towards Enlightenment, the state of total and complete awareness.

To reach Enlightenment, one needs the necessary Wisdom to make the correct choices (as shown in Figure 6).

To have wisdom, one must have the knowing. Knowledge is often mistaken for the knowing. Here knowledge is defined as a cerebral understanding; while knowing comes after an experience. Therefore, to attain a *knowing,* one needs the experience of life.

However, to have an experience, one needs time. And this is where we get stuck. We are told that there is only 24 hours a day for everyone.

However, time is relative! We can *slow down* the passage of time. There are two ways to slow down the time. The first is by suffering.

Suffering slows down time so that one can jam pack many days of experience into just a few hours. Anyone who has been in a *hot seat* knows that mere one minute on a hot seat feels like an hour. In a practical sense, that one minute *is* actually an hour.

But one can't use suffering as the only way to reach the Enlightenment. Each Suffering yields both a *knowing* and also a *scar*. This is because suffering is only a mimic, not the real thing. The real thing is Presence.

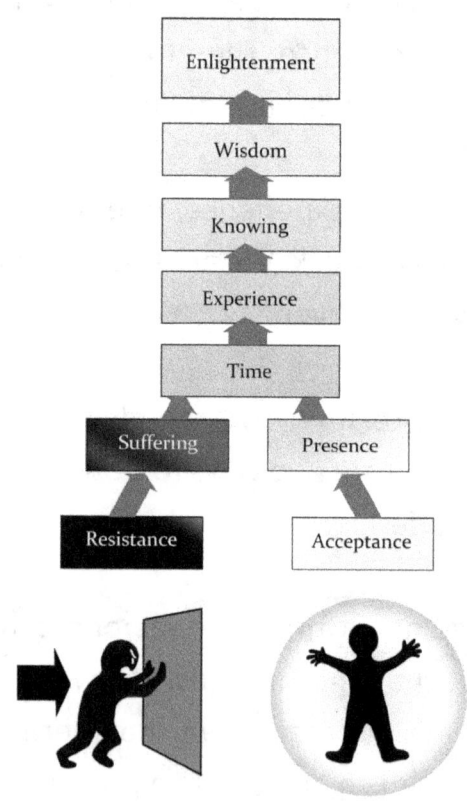

Figure 6. The Path to Enlightenment.

Cultivating the Presence

Presence is a natural state of being when the physical body, emotional body, mental body and spirit body all come into a straight-line alignment.

Presence = (Body + "Heart" + Mind + Spirit) alignment.

The Disintegrated Self (Figure 7) is the result when a person is emotionally weighed down by the traumas of the past, while at the same time imagines in the mind the worst possible future scenarios that directly threaten his life or lifestyle. Diagram below shows how a Disintegrated Self forms.

Disintegrated Self

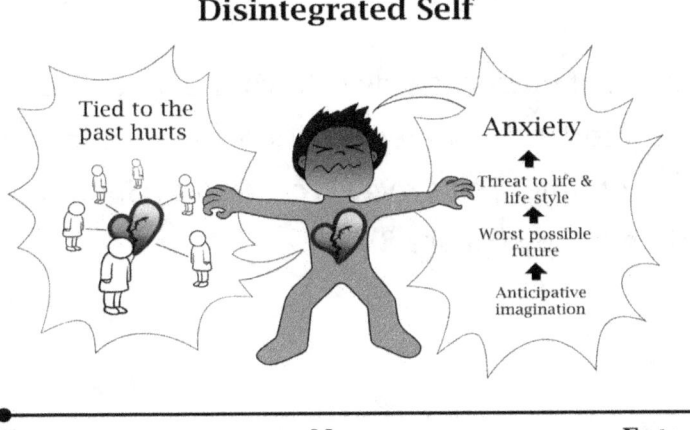

Presence occurs when an individual's past hurts are allowed to mature into just "another of his or her life experiences"—albeit important ones. Thus, the "heart" is relieved of the burdens and returns to the Being to avail itself as the pure state of feeling.

In order to have presence, the mind also has shed the weight of anxiety coming from the worst possible anticipations of the future, and returns to the Being to avail itself as the pure state of awareness.

When the Heart and the Mind come to the Now as pure feeling and awareness, a conducive environment is created for the Body and Spirit to enter. Presence is then the *4-bodies-in-1 phenomenon* where they resonate as a single unit in harmony.

This state of Presence slows down the time, allowing for the deeper and wider experiences of life in short periods of time. The syzygy is created by Spirit, Mind, Heart and Body (Figure 8).

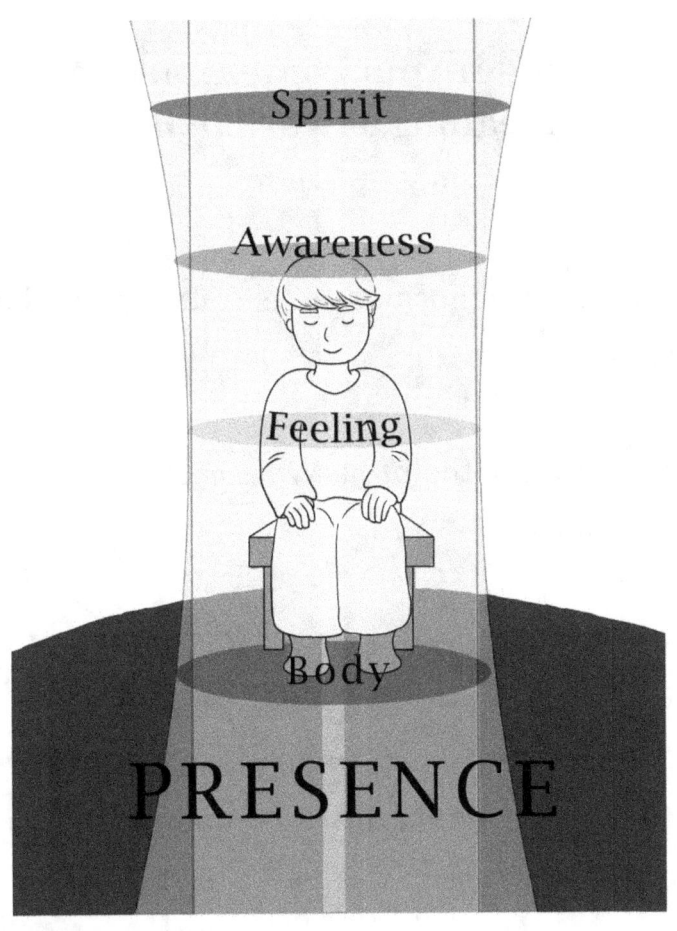

Figure 8. The Spirit, Mind, Heart and Body in syzygy.

In Presence, time slows down, allowing for greater experience in much shorter periods of time. This leads to greater knowings, which leads to wisdom. And when wisdom accumulates and reaches the critical threshold, one Awakens.

Prayer for your contentment and meaning at work in life.

May you see the enormous gifts contained in the present moment.

May you practice the *proactive* acceptance by making choices.

May you therefore, accept the Now.

Then discover the whole untapped world of possibilities that reside within this split moment that only a person of *Presence* may experience.

May you go out into the world with your invisible cup in your hands, collecting those precious thing that can lead to achieving the purpose why you originally crossed over from the Other World to Earth.

I.
THE UNHAPPY
STONECUTTER

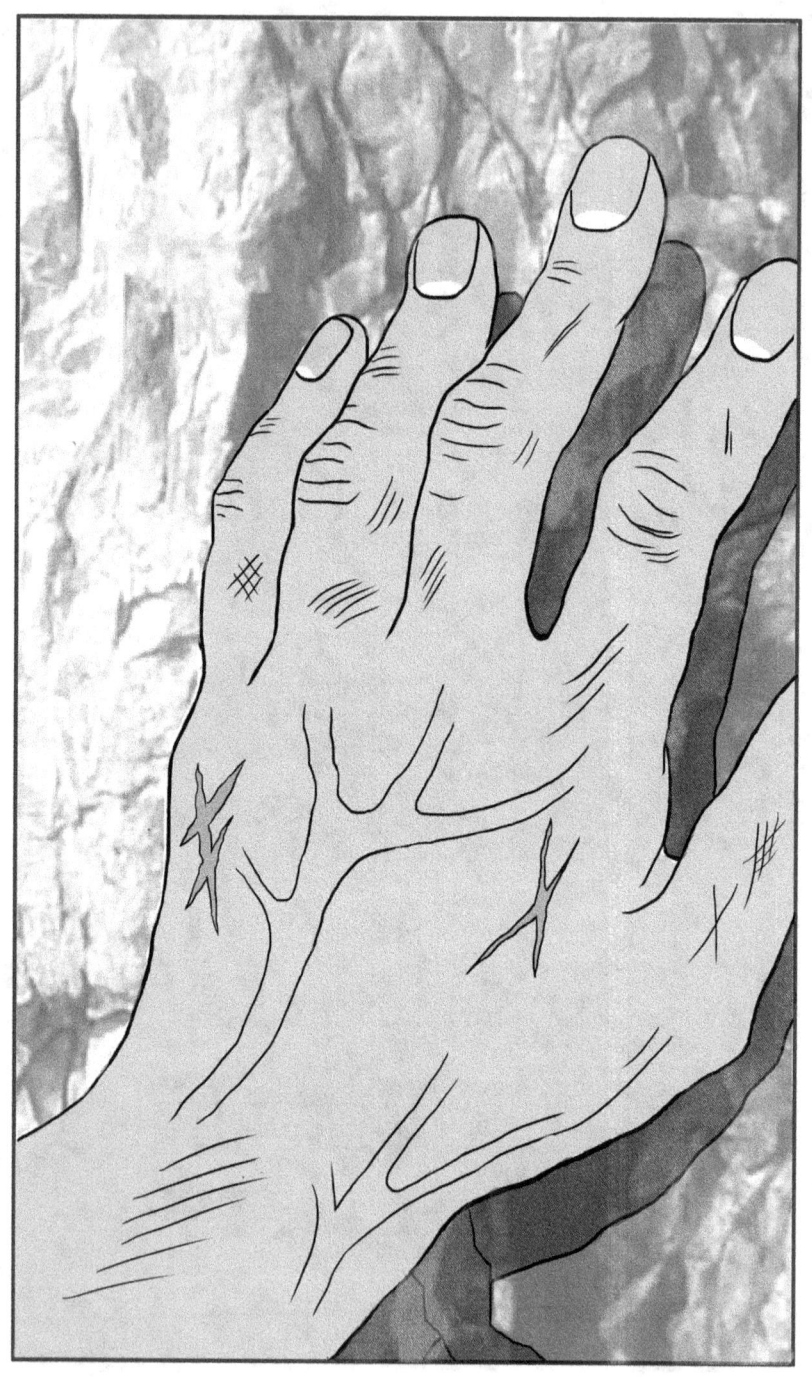

A long, long time ago, a man lived in Rome. His name was Tiberius, and he was a master stonecutter.

For many years he worked with rocks, and his hands became calloused and sore. The more he worked on the rocks, the rougher his hands became. Yet those rough hands created the most exquisite stone statues.

One day, Tiberius was exhausted. He worked many hours under the hot sun. He became distracted. It didn't take long before his chisel slipped and put a chip on the statue's eye.

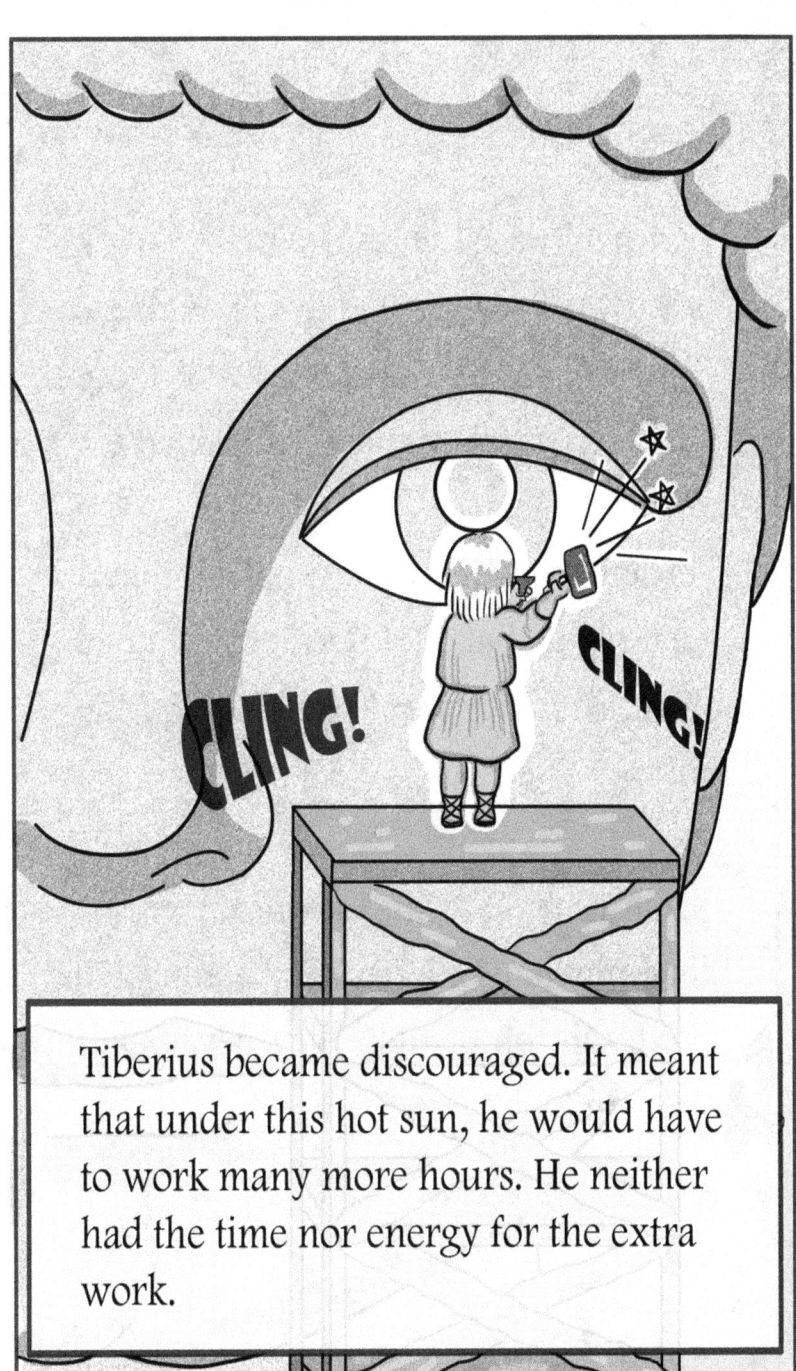

Tiberius became discouraged. It meant that under this hot sun, he would have to work many more hours. He neither had the time nor energy for the extra work.

It wasn't just the nature of the work that was hard. He had to deal with the customers! His customers were more unforgiving than the work itself.

When the work was complete, they'd complain that the work wasn't done right, and they would quibble over the price.

Each time, Tiberius ended up receiving only half of what had been promised. On top of that, they never paid him on time.

Tiberius went to the Wealthy Merchant's home to give a work estimate. When he opened the gate, he was welcomed by heavenly music and the most delicious aroma of food.

A celebration was going on. The guests were dressed up in the finest clothing.

The food. The music. The clothing. The refinement. Seeing what others had, Tiberius became dissatisfied with his social status.

At that very moment, a memory of an odd event entered his mind. It was a chance encounter with a spiritual master.

During his apprenticeship years, Tiberius spent months in Nazareth.

Nazareth was the mecca for aspiring apprentices who wished to hone their masonry skills. Here there was easy access to an abundance of limestone to work with.

It was here that he learned of a spiritual master. People flocked to him in order to find answers.

Tiberius remembered the Master well because of his soft and gentle voice.

The master said that people were essentially born with good nature. But it was their habits that turned one person into a saint and another into a thief.

Tiberius closed his eyes. He decided to still his heart. He let go of the emotional anchors to the past traumas.

He called back his heart in its purest state, feeling.

Tiberius decided to still his mind. His mind kept imagining negative futures, and became anxious. He stopped anticipating the future. He called back his mind in its purest state, awareness.

With the return of his feeling and awareness back to his body, his own spirit came back. Now he was fully present in the Now.

In this full presence, he prayed and believed that he was the Wealthy Merchant.

Stonecutter

II.
THE WEALTHY
MERCHANT

When the stonecutter opened his eyes, he was holding the merchant's golden goblet!!!

This is Amazing!!!

He saw beautiful women and handsome men dressed in their best attire. All of his cultured guests were looking at him with absolute admiration.

Most of all, he noticed his sore and calloused hands were no longer. They were replaced by a pair of soft hands that never had seen a day of hard labor.

Tiberius went to the market to conduct his daily business. Recognizing Tiberius, the shopkeepers came running and bowed to him.

Suddenly from a distance, he heard the trumpet blaring.

He saw the Emperor on top of a fierce war elephant. The soldiers marching ahead said out loud,

"Emperor's Coming!
Bow down on the ground!"

Tiberius forgot all the wonderful things that made him feel good about being the Wealthy Merchant. Now he was miserable.

I want to be the Emperor!!!

Once again, Tiberius closed his eyes.
He stilled his heart and mind.
Then he prayed and believed,

"I AM the Emperor!"

Stonecutter

III.
THE EMPEROR

When he opened his eyes, he was sitting on top of the elephant, holding onto the golden staff. He was the Emperor!

No one spoke a word in fear and respect
for their ultimate ruler.
How powerful Tiberius felt!

He said to himself,

"Why was I so content being a mere merchant? Look at all those wealthy merchants. They fear me so much that they can't even look at me. All their money means nothing."

Tiberius the Emperor traveled everywhere proudly on the fierce elephant.

The fun of the being the Emperor was suddenly interruped by the intense heat of the Sun. It was a hot day!

Again, Tiberius returned to the Presence.

He prayed that he was the Sun.
He believed that he was the Sun.

He thanked the universe for making this happen.

Stonecutter

IV.
THE SUN

When Tiberius opened his eyes,
he was the Sun!

Tiberius was amazed by his own light radiating from every pore of his body. "I'm enlightened!"

Tiberius was looking down on Earth. To him, everyone looked like ants crawling about. He began to send out intense heat. Some passed out.

However, Tiberius was too busy testing his new power and had no time to reflect upon his behavior.

He dried up the lakes and rivers, just because he could. Thousands of people suffered from heat-stroke and dehydration.

He burned up the whole fields.

In their suffering, people began to form religions.

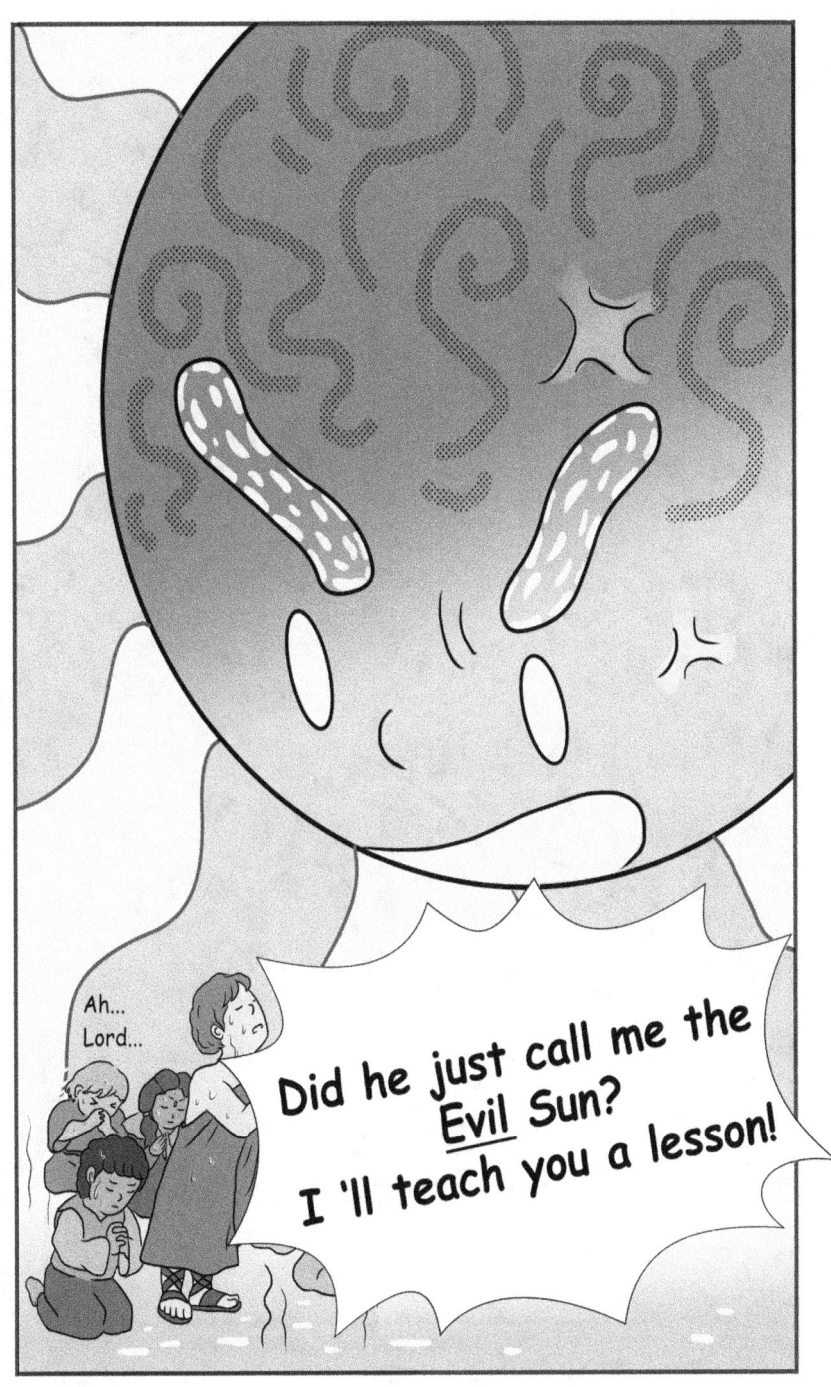

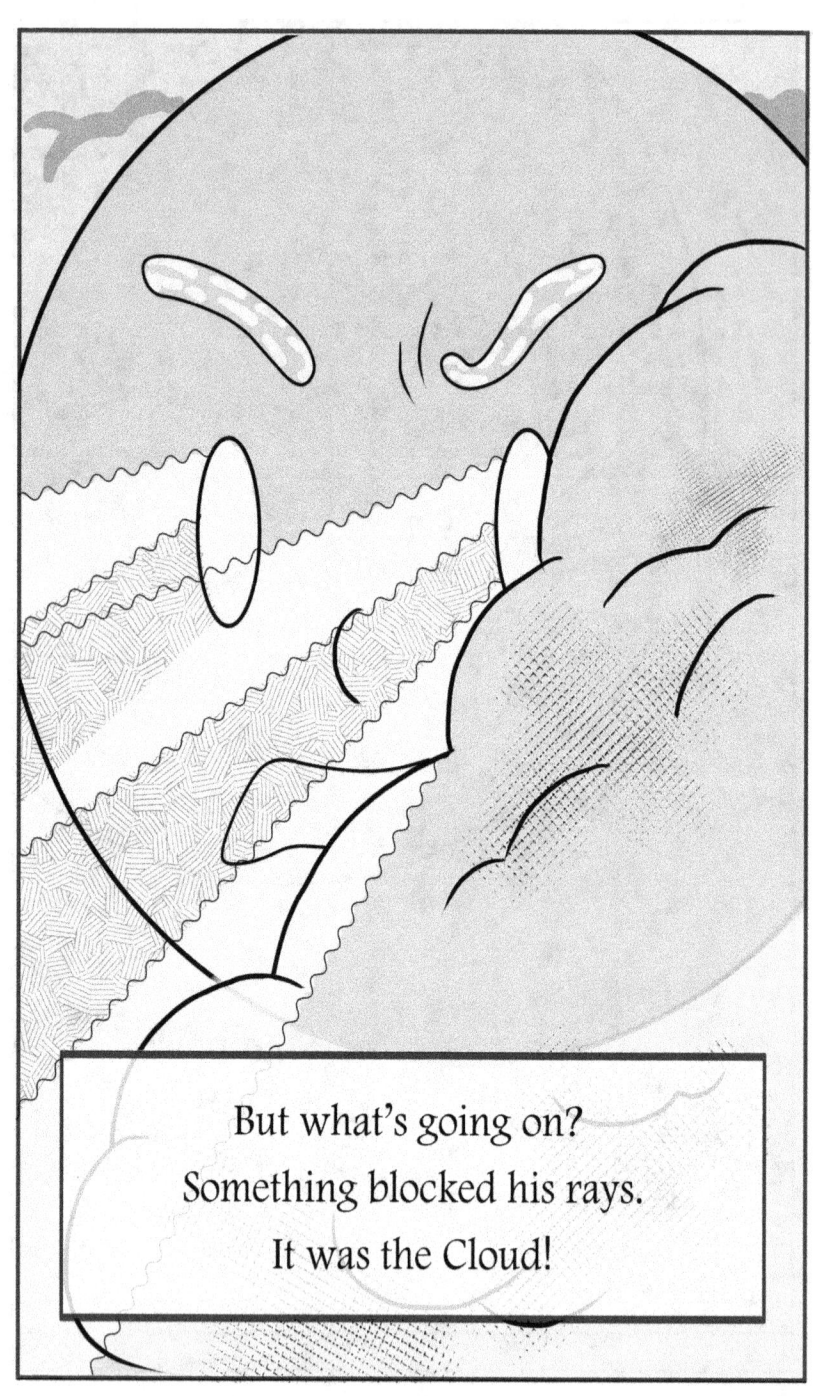

But what's going on?
Something blocked his rays.
It was the Cloud!

The Cloud sprinkled gentle rain upon the fields, wells, and rivers! The suffering came to an end. Everyone danced in joy!

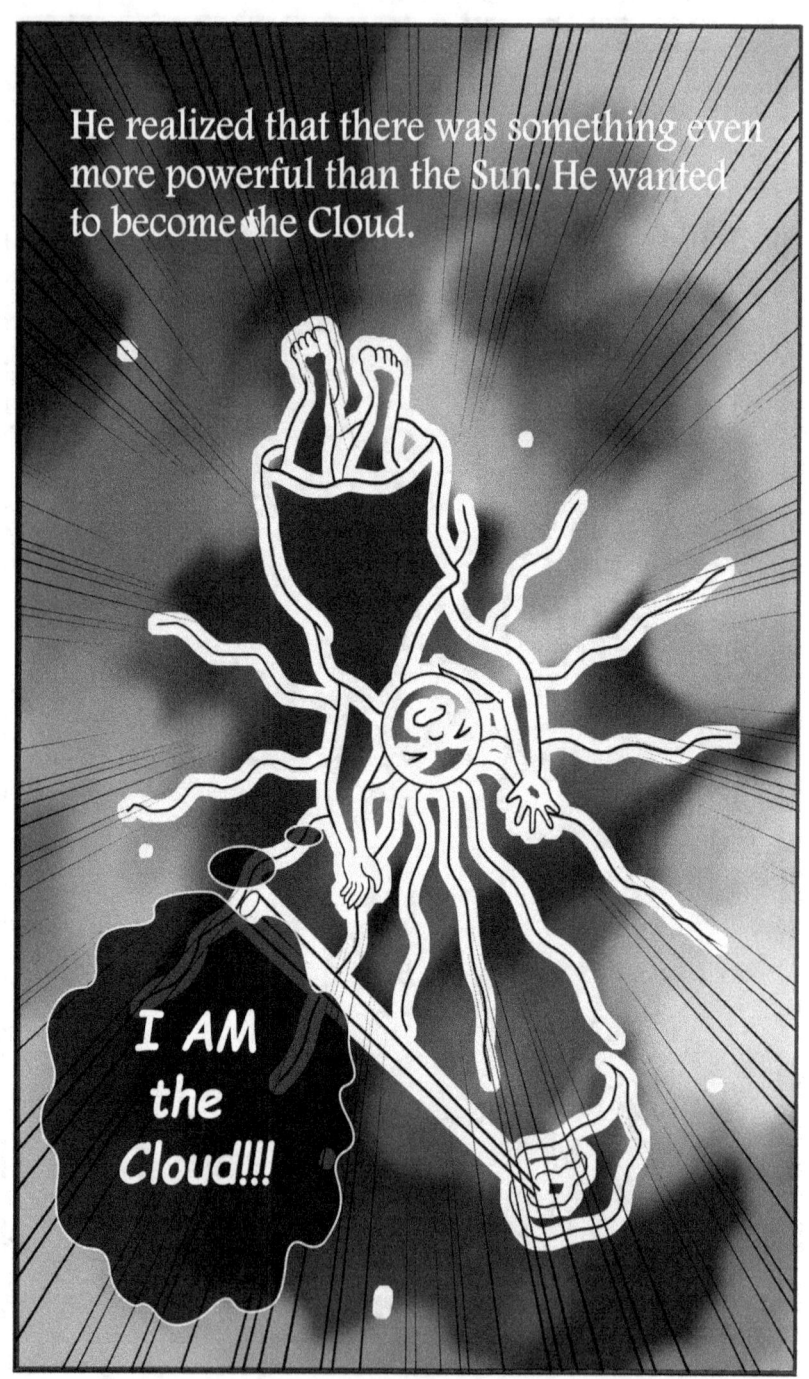

V.
THE CLOUD

He soaked up the Earth, and all that water destroyed everything in its path.

Suddenly, Tiberius felt that he was being pushed around. It was the Wind!!! He was suprised by the power of the Wind.

He was right.
The Wind can blow away anything.

"Why didn't I think of that?"
he thought.

Tiberius returned to his Presensce
again. He Prayed and Believed that
he was the Wind.

Stonecutter

VI.
THE WIND

When he opened his eyes, he was the Wind. He was as light as a leaf.

But his power was greater than ever
before. He could blow away anything.
So he blew away houses, horses, and
even great trees!

Tiberius the Wind found his new power to be fun. He could do anything.

From a distance, he saw the Giant Rock.
It was standing tall and proud.

Tiberius the Wind blew at the rock.
But the rock remained.

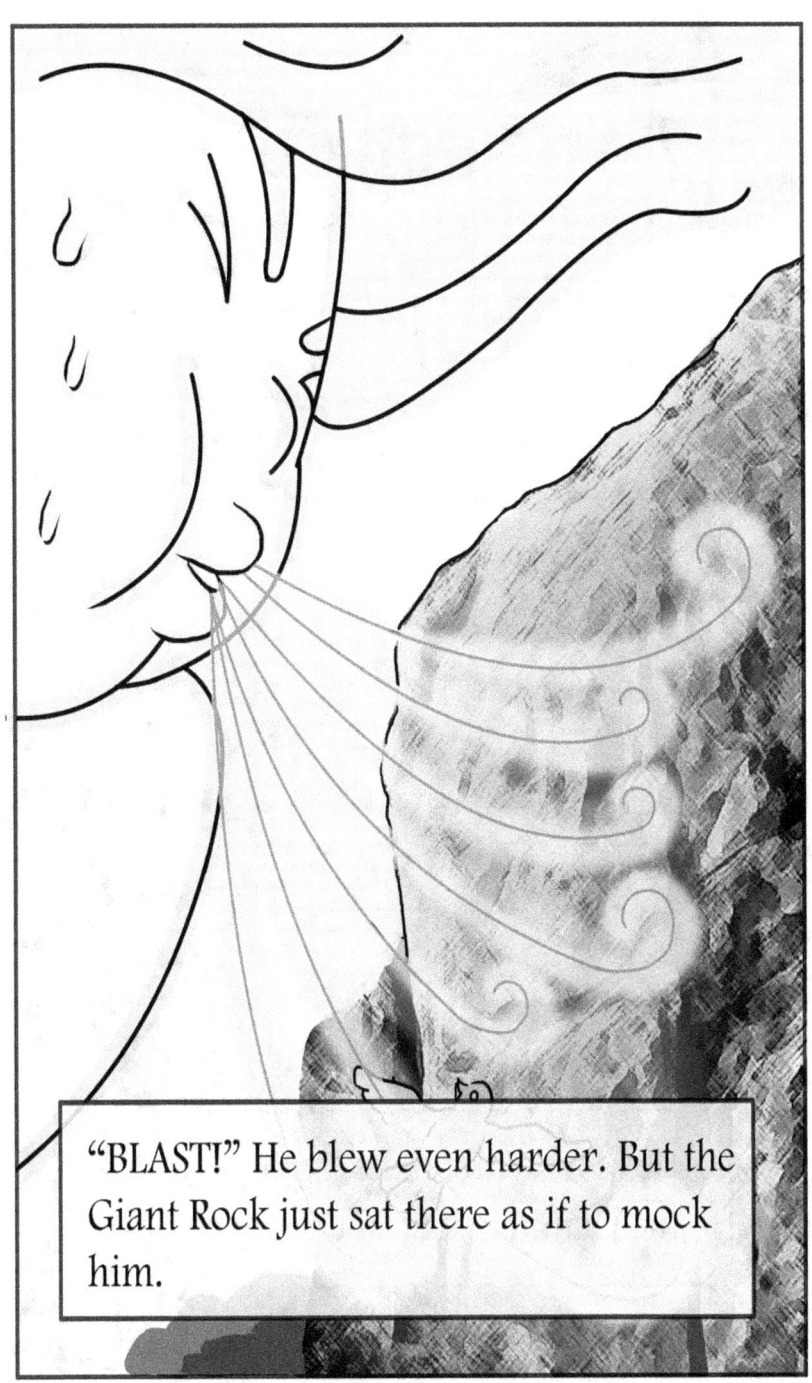

"BLAST!" He blew even harder. But the Giant Rock just sat there as if to mock him.

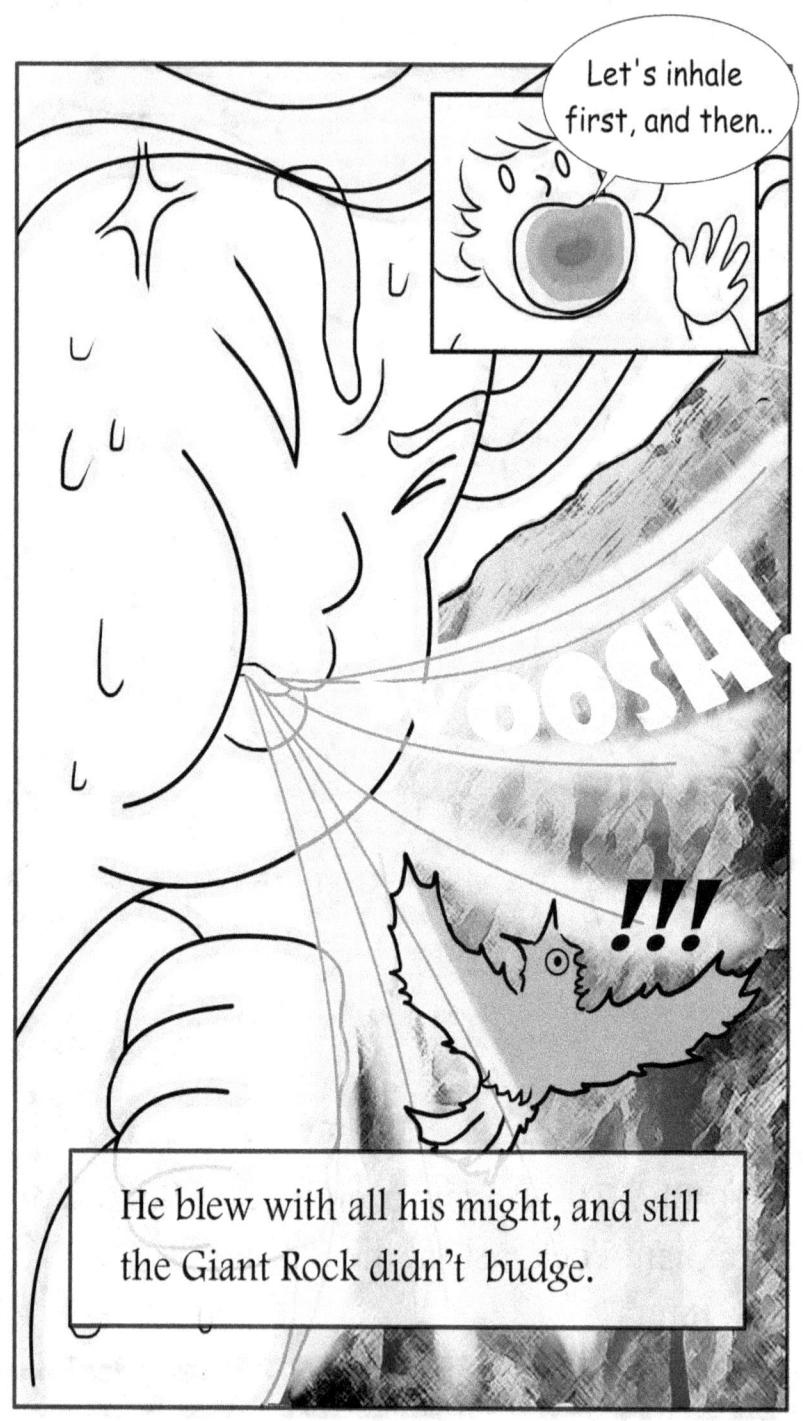

He blew with all his might, and still the Giant Rock didn't budge.

Thank you...

Once again he returned to the state of Presence. He Prayed and Believed that he was the Giant Rock.

Stonecutter

VII.
THE GIANT ROCK

When he opened his eyes, he was the Giant Rock. He sat there, proud. Tiberius was content that he was the most powerful of all. Finally!!!

He was more powerful than anything else. More powerful than the Wind, the Cloud, the Sun, the Emperor, and the Wealthy Merchant. He was content.

Stonecutter

VIII.

THE HAPPY
STONECUTTER

He kept climbing up the steps of power, only to find someone more powerful than him one step ahead.

Tiberius never was content for longer periods of time. As soon as he achieved his goal, he was content for only a brief moment, then he became discontented. And now, he saw his pattern. And he saw the cause of all this.

He closed his eyes, and he saw in the center of his mind, a tree that cast dark shadow.

Being at peace with himself, the Tree of Burden no longer served him a function. With his embrace, the tree withered and vaporized into thin air.

The dark shadow was no longer.
Instead brilliance was everywhere.

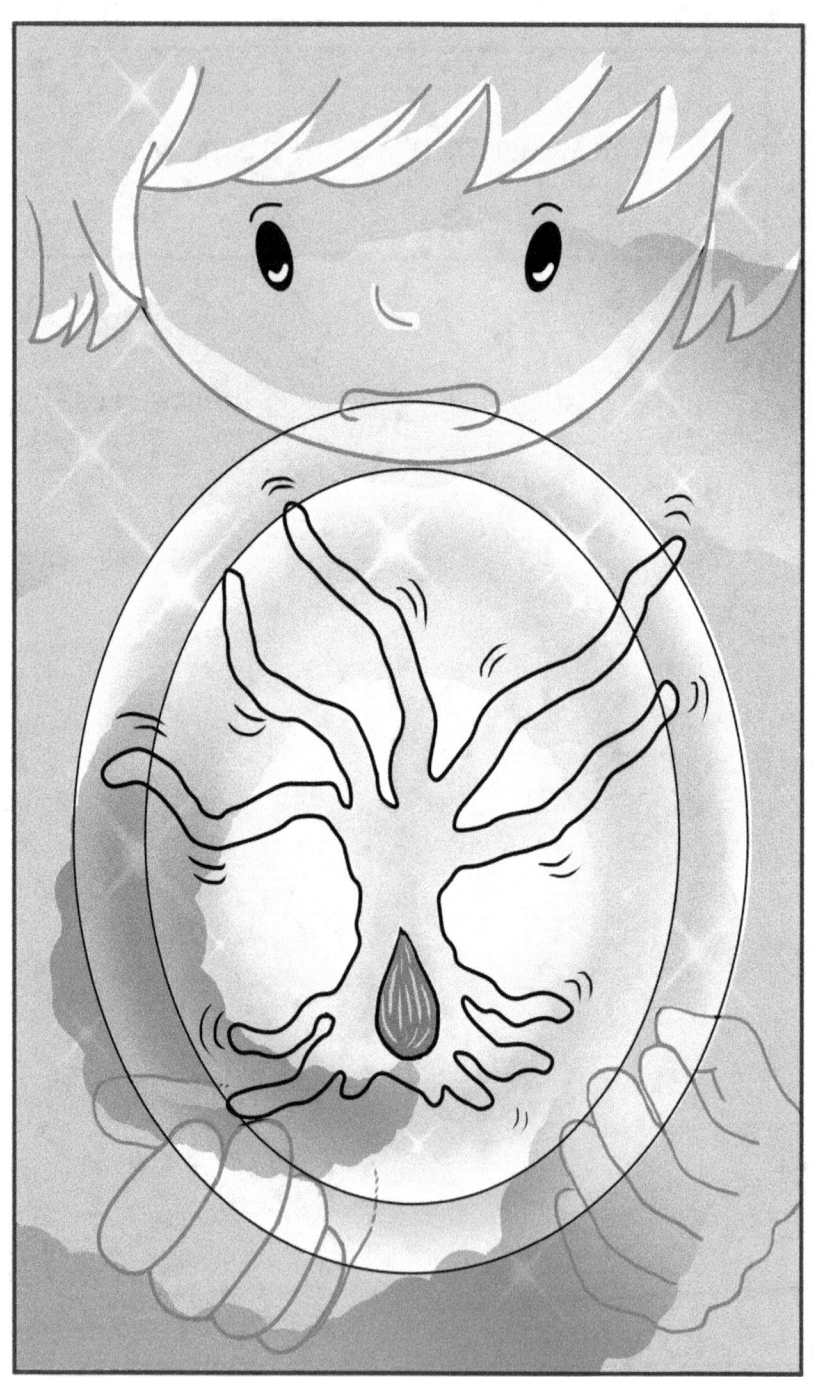

The seed began growing. Tiberius saw that it was the Tree of Life!

It's a new start. I will make this work.

Tiberius and the Tree of Life became one.

This Life...

Ah,
so beautiful...

Tiberius saw that the world was beauty itself.

Tiberius recalled when he walked side-by-side with his spiritual master.

They walked along the Sea of Galilee.

The Sky!

Déjà vu! He had this feeling of light-ness and presence when he was just a child.

It was a particularly starry night when his mom and dad took him up on the butte. And the three of them looked at the stars.

His life was simple.

He was present.

And all he felt was love surrounding him.

His face made a smile.

He wasn't trying to smile.

His face made the smile.

He returned to the simple innocence
once again.

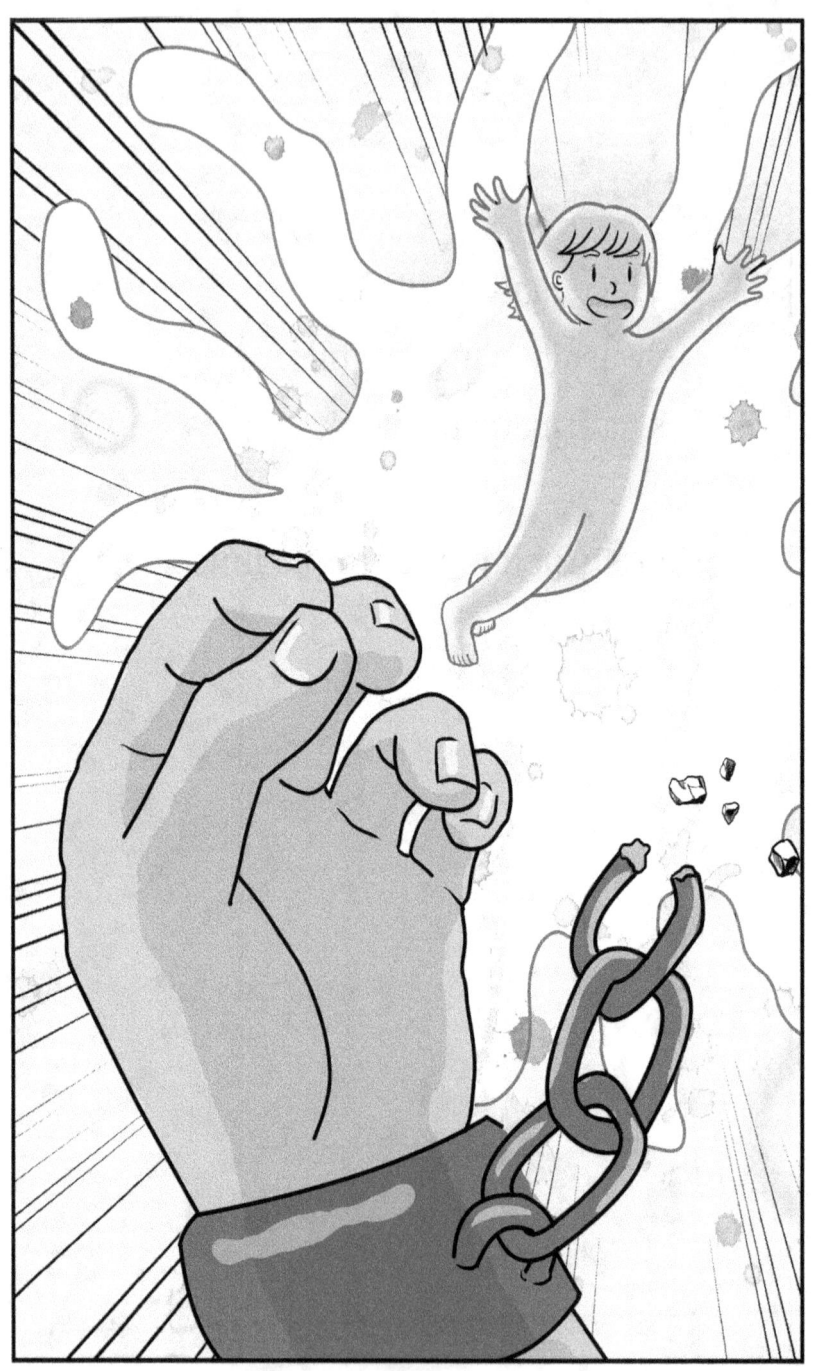

He felt liberated.
He was finally free from distractions.

Tiberius opened his eyes to the cool
breeze that wiped away the sweat on his
forehead. He put down his hammer and
chisel and settled his body in a cool
shade.

Tomorrow, he'll start a new project. it won't be for money. It won't be for recognition. It won't be for power. It will come straight from his Soul, shaped by the wisdom of his profound experience.

Tiberius saw the sun gently setting beyond the mountains.

And the sun set without him feeling anxious about tomorrow!

Tiberius came down, took a seat among his friends, and tasted the wine that was offered to him. It was soothing for his hard-worked muscles.

Romanus played his cithara, always sweet and always touching. And Marcus started singing. And everyone else began to sing along.

Tiberius saw his friends' noble faces. He knew well that every single one of them were fighting great personal battles within.

Yet their songs of joy echoed throughout the land, giving life to the waters and the mountains. In their presence, they became content.

Stonecutter

Epilogue

In the state of presence, discontentment will be re-solved, and meaning reclaimed. In that state, one ascends towards Enlightenment.

I believe that in the near future, linear thinking will fall out of favor, replaced by holistic thinking. In that future, the CEO may choose to come back to the company as the head security guard. In that future, the professors return to the university volunteering in the library or bookstore to guide those students who need clarity and inspiration. In that future, the prime ministers and presidents may choose to come back to public service as activists for the underdogs.

Yet they would feel content, and their lives replete with meaning.

www.ingramcontent.com/pod-product-compliance
Lightning Source LLC
Chambersburg PA
CBHW072304200526

45168CB00014B/405